PAUL ROMANUK

HOCKEY SUPERSTARS 2020-2021

D1370411

Author's Note

Last season was one of the strangest NHL seasons ever! It ended before any of us expected, and getting it restarted was full of question marks. You will notice, looking through this year's edition of *Hockey Superstars*, that we don't have all of the award winners listed or any information about the Stanley Cup playoffs. This is because when this book had to be printed, there was still no definite plan for the playoffs, and many of the award winners had yet to be announced. And since we didn't know exactly when the new season would start, you may have to adjust the dates in the fill-in pages yourself. What we do know is that there are still some great stories to tell about some of your favorite players. We hope you enjoy reading them.

For all of the up-to-date information about the end of last season — award winners, draft picks and more — you can visit us at www.scholastic.ca/hockey-superstars.

Happy hockey watching!

—Paul

SCHOLASTIC

TORONTO NEW YORK LONDON AUCKLAND SYDNEY
MEXICO CITY NEW DELHI HONG KONG BUENOS AIRES

THE TEAMS

WESTERN CONFERENCE – PACIFIC DIVISION

CALGARY FLAMES
team colors: red, gold, black and white
home arena: Scotiabank Saddledome
mascot: Harvey the Hound
Stanley Cups won: 1

EDMONTON OILERS
team colors: white, royal blue and orange
home arena: Rogers Place
mascot: Hunter
Stanley Cups won: 5

ANAHEIM DUCKS
team colors: black, gold, orange and white
home arena: Honda Center
mascot: Wild Wing
Stanley Cups won: 1

LOS ANGELES KINGS
team colors: white, black and silver
home arena: Staples Center
mascot: Bailey
Stanley Cups won: 2

ARIZONA COYOTES
team colors: red, black, sand and white
home arena: Gila River Arena
mascot: Howler

VANCOUVER CANUCKS
team colors: blue, silver, green and white
home arena: Rogers Arena
mascot: Fin

SAN JOSE SHARKS
team colors: teal, black, orange and white
home arena: SAP Center at San Jose
mascot: S.J. Sharkie

VEGAS GOLDEN KNIGHTS
team colors: steel gray, gold, red and black
home arena: T-Mobile Arena
mascot: Chance

WESTERN CONFERENCE – CENTRAL DIVISION

CHICAGO BLACKHAWKS
nickname: Hawks
team colors: red, black and white
home arena: United Center
mascot: Tommy Hawk
Stanley Cups won: 6

COLORADO AVALANCHE
nickname: Avs
team colors: burgundy, silver, black, blue and white
home arena: Pepsi Center
mascot: Bernie
Stanley Cups won: 2

DALLAS STARS
team colors: green, white, black and silver
home arena: American Airlines Center
mascot: Victor E. Green
Stanley Cups won: 1

NASHVILLE PREDATORS
nickname: Preds
team colors: dark blue, white and gold
home arena: Bridgestone Arena
mascot: Gnash

MINNESOTA WILD
team colors: red, green, gold, wheat and white
home arena: Xcel Energy Center
mascot: Nordy

WINNIPEG JETS
team colors: dark blue, blue, gray, silver, red and white
home arena: Bell MTS Place
mascot: Mick E. Moose

ST. LOUIS BLUES
team colors: blue, gold, dark blue and white
home arena: Enterprise Center
mascot: Louie
Stanley Cups won: 1

Stanley Cups won are as of July 2020

EASTERN CONFERENCE – ATLANTIC DIVISION

TORONTO MAPLE LEAFS
nickname: Leafs
team colors: blue and white
home arena: Scotiabank Arena
mascot: Carlton the Bear
Stanley Cups won: 11

BUFFALO SABRES
team colors: navy blue, gold, silver and white
home arena: KeyBank Center
mascot: Sabretooth

FLORIDA PANTHERS
nickname: Cats
team colors: red, navy blue, yellow, gold and white
home arena: BB&T Center
mascots: Stanley C. Panther and Viktor E. Ratt

OTTAWA SENATORS
nickname: Sens
team colors: black, red, gold and white
home arena: Canadian Tire Centre
mascot: Spartacat

TAMPA BAY LIGHTNING
nickname: Bolts
team colors: blue, black and white
home arena: Amalie Arena
mascot: ThunderBug
Stanley Cups won: 1

MONTREAL CANADIENS
nickname: Habs
team colors: red, blue and white
home arena: Bell Centre
mascot: Youppi
Stanley Cups won: 24

DETROIT RED WINGS
nickname: Wings
team colors: red and white
home arena: Little Caesars Arena
mascot (unofficial): Al the Octopus
Stanley Cups won: 11

BOSTON BRUINS
nickname: Bs
team colors: gold, black and white
home arena: TD Garden
mascot: Blades
Stanley Cups won: 6

EASTERN CONFERENCE – METROPOLITAN DIVISION

NEW YORK RANGERS
nickname: Blueshirts
team colors: blue, white and red
home arena: Madison Square Garden
Stanley Cups won: 4

COLUMBUS BLUE JACKETS
nickname: Jackets
team colors: blue, red, silver and white
home arena: Nationwide Arena
mascot: Stinger

WASHINGTON CAPITALS
nickname: Caps
team colors: red, navy blue and white
home arena: Capital One Arena
mascot: Slapshot
Stanley Cups won: 1

NEW YORK ISLANDERS
nickname: Isles
team colors: orange, blue and white
home arena: Barclays Center and Nassau Coliseum
mascot: Sparky the Dragon
Stanley Cups won: 4

PITTSBURGH PENGUINS
nickname: Pens
team colors: black, gold and white
home arena: PPG Paints Arena
mascot: Iceburgh
Stanley Cups won: 5

PHILADELPHIA FLYERS
team colors: orange, white and black
home arena: Wells Fargo Center
mascot: Gritty
Stanley Cups won: 2

NEW JERSEY DEVILS
team colors: red, black and white
home arena: Prudential Center
mascot: N.J. Devil
Stanley Cups won: 3

CAROLINA HURRICANES
nickname: Canes
team colors: red, black, gray and white
home arena: PNC Arena
mascot: Stormy and Caroline
Stanley Cups won: 1

YOUR FAVORITE TEAM

Name of your favorite team: _____

Conference and division: _____

Players on your favorite team at the start of the season:

Number	Name	Position
_____	_____	_____
_____	_____	_____
_____	_____	_____
_____	_____	_____
_____	_____	_____
_____	_____	_____
_____	_____	_____
_____	_____	_____
_____	_____	_____
_____	_____	_____
_____	_____	_____
_____	_____	_____
_____	_____	_____

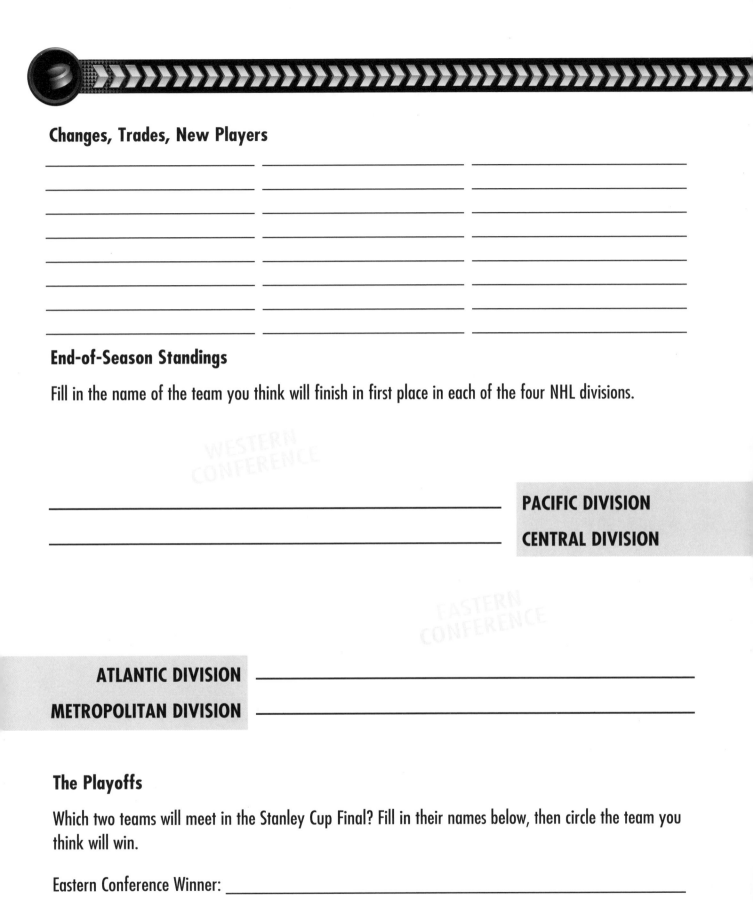

Changes, Trades, New Players

_____ _____ _____
_____ _____ _____
_____ _____ _____
_____ _____ _____
_____ _____ _____
_____ _____ _____
_____ _____ _____

End-of-Season Standings

Fill in the name of the team you think will finish in first place in each of the four NHL divisions.

WESTERN CONFERENCE

_____ **PACIFIC DIVISION**

_____ **CENTRAL DIVISION**

EASTERN CONFERENCE

ATLANTIC DIVISION _____

METROPOLITAN DIVISION _____

The Playoffs

Which two teams will meet in the Stanley Cup Final? Fill in their names below, then circle the team you think will win.

Eastern Conference Winner: _____

Western Conference Winner: _____

YOUR FAVORITE TEAM

Your Team — All Season Long

The standings of hockey teams are listed at NHL.com and on the sports pages of the newspaper all season long. The standings will show you which team is in first place, second place, etc., right down to last place.

Some of the abbreviations you'll become familiar with are: GP for games played; W for wins; L for losses; OT for overtime losses; PTS for points; A for assists; G for goals.

Check the standings on the same day of every month and copy down what they say about your team. By keeping track of your team this way you'll be able to see when it was playing well and when it wasn't.

	GP	W	L	OT	PTS
NOVEMBER 1					
DECEMBER 1					
JANUARY 1					
FEBRUARY 1					
MARCH 1					
APRIL 1					
MAY 1					

Final Standings

At the end of the season print the final record of your team below.

YOUR TEAM	GP	W	L	OT	PTS

Your Favorite Players' Scoring Records

While you're keeping track of your favorite team during the season, you can also follow the progress of your favorite players. Just fill in their point totals on the same day of every month.

player	nov 1	dec 1	jan 1	feb 1	mar 1	apr 1	may 1

Your Favorite Goaltenders' Records

You can keep track of your favorite goaltenders' averages during the season. Just fill in the information below.

GAA is the abbreviation for goals-against average. That's the average number of goals given up by a goaltender during a game over the course of the season.

goaltender	nov 1	dec 1	jan 1	feb 1	mar 1	apr 1	may 1

JORDAN BINNINGTON

ST. LOUIS BLUES

The sports world is full of fairy tales: A Canadian kid scoring the once-in-a-lifetime, Olympic-gold-medal-winning goal in his home country (Sidney Crosby, 2010). The practice goalie and part-time Zamboni driver who suddenly finds himself in an NHL game, helping his team to the win (David Ayres, last season). And, of course, the 2019 march to the Stanley Cup by the St. Louis Blues, led by goaltender Jordan Binnington.

On January 1, 2019, the Blues were in last place in the league. On January 7, Jordan, recently recalled from the minors, started his first NHL game. He shut out Philadelphia 3–0 and took over as the team's number one goalie. The Blues then went on a remarkable run, winning 15 of their next 20 games — including putting together a franchise record 11-game winning streak. St. Louis made the playoffs and won the Stanley Cup, and Jordan became a hero. What a story.

But even with that level of success, Jordan knew that his NHL career was only beginning. He didn't make his first NHL start until he was 25 years old. He put in a lot of time in the minors. While every player works hard to get to the NHL, Jordan had to work hard *and* wait for his chance. He'd have to prove that he wasn't a fluke, a one-hit wonder.

"I wasn't done [after the Cup win]. I had a lot to prove for myself, for my family. I felt like I deserved to be here. I had to learn a few things and gain some experience and just figure more out about myself. I think that comes with age."

"Stuff gets said," acknowledged Jordan at the All-Star Game in 2020, "and you just can't listen to it. I've just got to prepare and be the best goaltender I can with my time here. It's been successful so far."

Jordan picked up last season right where he left off during the Blues' championship run. Aside from being selected to go to the All-Star Game, he finished third in the league with 30 wins in the shortened NHL season.

"I wanted to be in the NHL by the time I was 20, 21, 22, 23 . . . and it wasn't working out," recalls Jordan. "When I got my opportunity, I had to be ready. I wasn't ever going to take playing in the NHL for granted, even after we'd won the Cup."

DID YOU KNOW?

Jordan is only the sixth goalie in NHL history to earn his 40th career win prior to his 60th game. He picked up win number 40 in his 56th start, on December 16, 2019, against Colorado.

HOCKEY MEMORIES

Jordan's goaltending debut came by accident. He was seven years old and waiting to play a 3-on-3 game. The goalie hadn't shown up. They asked for a volunteer and Jordan stepped up.

2019–2020 STATS

GP	W	L	OT	GAA	SO
50	30	13	7	2.56	3

St. Louis Blues' 4th choice, 88th overall, in 2011 NHL Entry Draft

1st NHL Team, Season: St. Louis Blues, 2018–2019

Born: July 11, 1993, in Richmond Hill, Ontario

Position: Goaltender

Catches: Left

Height: 1.85 m (6'1")

Weight: 79 kg (174 lbs.)

JOHN CARLSON

In 2012 Nicklas Lidstrom, the greatest defenseman of his era, hung up his skates for the last time. Since Lidstrom retired, great defensemen like Erik Karlsson, Drew Doughty and Brent Burns have all provided hockey fans with many moments of brilliant play. Last season Washington's John Carlson stepped into the spotlight.

John put up the best numbers of his career and led all NHL defensemen in scoring. He has actually been the top points-producing defenseman in the NHL over the last three seasons, with 43 goals and 170 assists for 213 points. While some hockey fans may not have noticed John prior to the last couple of seasons, his great play was nothing new to Washington fans. He's spent his entire career with the Caps.

"You just try to go out there on the ice and do your thing, knowing that every moment in that game could be a big deal. You want to be on the right side of that moment."
— John on playoff hockey

"He's a horse for us and has been for a few years now," says fellow Cap Tom Wilson. "He's just so steady. He doesn't go end-to-end or anything like that, he just gets the job done. He has great offensive ability. Not flashy. He does his thing."

By just "doing his thing" John has become the highest-scoring defenseman in Washington franchise history. The record-setting point came on February 23, 2020, against the Penguins, when he picked up an assist. It was the 475th point of his career, beating the record held by long-time Caps defenseman Calle Johansson.

"It's great," said John. "I've been here for a while, and that definitely helps. I've been here during a stretch of probably the best players in the history of the franchise. There have been a lot of great factors for me and I'm glad to be a part of it."

John has played with the best players ever to wear the Caps sweater. But, make no mistake, his name also features prominently on any list of all-time Washington greats, as well as on any current list of sensational NHL defensemen.

DID YOU KNOW?
John has a lot of team hardware. He scored the championship-winning goal for Team USA at the 2010 World Junior Championships, was part of a Calder Cup Championship in 2010 and, of course, won a Stanley Cup with the Capitals in 2018.

HOCKEY MEMORIES
Although he was born in Massachusetts, John grew up in New Jersey. Some of his most special memories are of "some of the Devils players coming to our practice, and you'd get to see them up close and talk to them."

2019–2020 STATS

GP	G	A	PTS
69	15	60	75

Washington Capitals' 2nd choice, 27th overall, in 2008 NHL Entry Draft
1st NHL Team, Season: Washington Capitals, 2010–2011
Born: January 10, 1990, in Natick, Massachusetts
Position: Defense
Shoots: Right
Height: 1.90 m (6'3")
Weight: 98.5 kg (217 lbs.)

KYLE CONNOR

The start of last season was tough for Kyle Connor, as he held out during training camp before signing a seven-year contract extension. The holdout was tough for a couple of reasons.

"You have a great opportunity every time you step out there on the ice. Every shift, you have to go out there and prove yourself and play the best you can."

"As an athlete, you just want to be out there," said Kyle, after everything was settled. "I had a great off-season. A lot of weight training, and I worked on getting better all around with my game speed and strength. All those little things that make you successful."

Another aspect of Kyle's success is the mature outlook he maintained during his development. During the 2016-2017 NHL season he was sent down to the minors after 19 games. It was a surprise to many. Kyle was a star in his final season of college hockey and was named the Big Ten Player of the Year. Coming off that kind of success, many young players would have reacted badly to being demoted. Kyle didn't take that view.

"I was playing on the third line and playing maybe five minutes a night," recalls Kyle. "Being sent down was perfect for me. They [the Manitoba Moose] put me in all situations and I started playing really well and learned the pro game."

One of the important things Kyle learned during his stint in the minors was that you have to be all in, every shift, every night. There is a huge difference between a 30-to-40 game college season and the grind of an 82-game NHL season (never mind playoffs). Lessons learned, he hit the ground running and hasn't stopped since. The numbers don't lie. Kyle is one of only 12 players in the league to have scored 100 or more goals over the last three seasons. He racked up his 200th career point in the final game of last year's shortened season, when he potted a couple of goals against the Edmonton Oilers.

Kyle started off last season under some pressure, but there will be a lot more pressure on the whole team to start this season. A Jets team loaded with some very good players is still waiting for a trip to the Final and a chance at the Stanley Cup.

DID YOU KNOW?

Kyle decided on sweater number 81 with the Jets when he discovered that his college number, 18, was already taken by Jets teammate Bryan Little. "At first I wasn't sure, but now I like 81 better than 18," he says.

HOCKEY MEMORIES

When Kyle was a kid, his dad, Joe, painted the basement floor of the family home to look like a rink. He even painted boards and fans on the walls! Kyle would slip on a pair of in-line skates and spend hours stickhandling and firing pucks for the pretend crowd.

2019–2020 STATS

GP	G	A	PTS
71	38	35	73

Winnipeg Jets' 1st choice, 17th overall, in 2015 NHL Entry Draft
1st NHL Team, Season: Winnipeg Jets, 2017–2018
Born: December 9, 1996, in Shelby Township, Michigan
Position: Left Wing
Shoots: Left
Height: 1.85 m (6'1")
Weight: 82.5 kg (182 lbs.)

LEON DRAISAITL

Leon Draisaitl is a major part of the future hopes of the Edmonton Oilers, but at least one person in the team's front office can't help but think of the past when he watches him play. Wayne Gretzky was half of one of the great duos in the history of the game. When he and Jari Kurri played together, it was as though they were seeing the game through the same set of eyes. During their eight seasons together in Edmonton in the 1980s, the two shared four Stanley Cup Championships while racking up a combined 2,380 points.

> "It's the best league in the world and the best players in the world play in it. It is so special for me to be a part of that."

Gretzky's on-ice career is long over. In his current management role with the Oilers he watches a lot of games, and when he watches Leon Draisaitl play alongside Connor McDavid, it takes Gretzky back to his days with Kurri.

"I can see similarities," says Gretzky. "You can see that they think the game the same way. They have a real chemistry. With us, when push came to shove, Jari was really the shooter of our pair. With these two, I see Leon as the shooter in many ways."

Leon has indeed done a lot of shooting, and scoring, during the last couple of seasons. He led the league during the shortened season with a career-best 110 points. His total of 93 goals over the last two seasons leads the Oilers and is second in the league only to Alex Ovechkin's 99. Leon seems to be able to find the open areas of the ice, the way Kurri could with Gretzky, and McDavid is able to get him the puck the way Gretzky could.

"I think we complement each other really well," says Leon. "We like playing with one another. We have great chemistry on the ice and we're good friends off the ice too."

Many great duos have played major roles in Stanley Cup Championships. In recent years, Ovechkin-Backstrom in Washington, Crosby-Malkin in Pittsburgh and Toews-Kane in Chicago have delivered consistently and won it all. That will always be a measure of greatness in the NHL, and that's the future Oilers fans are hoping for with McDavid and Draisaitl.

DID YOU KNOW?

Leon's dad is former German National Team player Peter Draisaitl. Leon learned to play the game in Cologne, where his dad played with the local team. Leon moved to Canada in 2012 to play with the Prince Albert Raiders of the Western Hockey League.

HOCKEY MEMORIES

October 3, 2018, is a day Leon will never forget. He suited up for the Oilers in a pre-season game in his hometown of Cologne, Germany, against the local team, Kölner Haie, coached by his dad. "It was an amazing and special night for me and my family," said Leon.

2019–2020 STATS

GP	G	A	PTS
71	43	67	110

Edmonton Oilers' 1st choice, 3rd overall, in 2014 NHL Entry Draft
1st NHL Team, Season: Edmonton Oilers, 2014–2015
Born: October 27, 1995, in Cologne, Germany
Position: Center
Shoots: Left
Height: 1.88 m (6'2")
Weight: 94.5 kg (208 lbs.)

JACK EICHEL

It's not hard to draw comparisons between Jack Eichel — the promise of a great future for today's Buffalo Sabres — and a man who symbolized Buffalo greatness in the team's early years. Superstar Gilbert Perreault was the team's first-ever draft pick, first overall, and is still Buffalo's all-time leader in games played, goals, assists and points. The first connection between the two players came in 2013, when Perreault saw Jack play for the USA in the World U17 Hockey Challenge, in Perreault's hometown of Victoriaville, Quebec. Jack got three goals in five games. But it wasn't just the goal-scoring that caught Perreault's eye.

"I like anything to do with a battle. Hockey is a game of different battles. If you win those, you will be successful."

"What impressed me at the time," recalls Perreault, "was his great skating ability, the way he could shoot the puck and the way he could make plays."

Last season with the Sabres all of those skills were on display. Jack led the team in scoring, put up a career-best 36 goals and was well on the way to the highest point total of his career before the season ended. And, say some who play against him, Jack's overall game was better.

"It takes some time to learn how important it is and how hard it is to play away from the puck," says Toronto Maple Leafs veteran John Tavares. "From what I've seen this year, he's getting better. He's one of the best players in the league."

Despite Jack's play, the Sabres haven't managed to make the playoffs since the young star arrived on the scene in 2015. It's worth remembering that a player can become a star in the NHL fairly quickly — if you're a high draft choice, have a great season or do something extraordinary. But it takes years to become a great NHL player. Gilbert Perreault, tagged as a star as first overall pick in 1970, didn't become a great player until several years later, as his game matured and the Sabres built a great team around him. The Sabres want to do the same with Jack Eichel.

"It takes time," says Perreault. "If he plays his whole career here [like I did] and doesn't get hurt, he'll get all the records."

DID YOU KNOW?

Jack began his NHL career wearing number 15. Number 9, which he wore in college hockey and for Team USA, belonged to then-teammate Evander Kane. After Kane was traded, Jack grabbed his old number back!

HOCKEY MEMORIES

During one of the NHL's outdoor Winter Classic games, Jack reflected on his dad, Bob, picking him up after school on Fridays and heading to a local frozen pond to play until it was dark. "That's where it started for me. Those are the roots of the game."

2019–2020 STATS

GP	G	A	PTS
68	36	42	78

Buffalo Sabres' 1st choice, 2nd overall, in 2015 NHL Entry Draft
1st NHL Team, Season: Buffalo Sabres, 2015–2016
Born: October 28, 1996, in North Chelmsford, Massachusetts
Position: Center
Shoots: Right
Height: 1.88 m (6'2")
Weight: 92 kg (203 lbs.)

CONNOR HELLEBUYCK

There were a lot of unfinished stories last season, and the one the Winnipeg Jets were writing was one of them. That story began in 2017–2018, when many pieces of a big puzzle were starting to fit together. Blake Wheeler exploded with a 91-point season, Patrik Laine had the best season of his career and Nikolaj Ehlers and Mark Scheifele took the next steps in their development. It was also the season that netminder Connor Hellebuyck took the reins as the Jets' number one goalie and started down a path towards being one of the best in the game. The Jets made it all the way to the Western Conference Final before falling to the Vegas Golden Knights.

The following season the Jets stumbled in the first round of the playoffs, so last season was supposed to be when they made good on the promise of 2018.

"He's a hyper-focused, competitive guy and he has a real desire to be elite. That's how he drives himself."
— Winnipeg Jets coach Paul Maurice

"Hungry to play is a good way to put it," said Connor early last season. "Look, this is a win-or-go-home league. If you want to be someone and stick around, you have to win."

The Jets were battling for a playoff spot when the 2019–2020 season was halted, so their story remained unfinished.

"I had that feeling that we had something special going and we were peaking at the right time," said Connor. "Everyone was starting to feel it in the locker room."

Connor maintained his spot as one of the top goalies in the NHL. He had six shut-outs, and among goalies with 40 or more starts, he had the second-best save percentage (.922). The team was on a mission, but he was on his own personal mission as well.

"Everything is coming together and I'm seeing a lot of the potential I have," said Connor last season. "Maybe I can make a push to be the best."

It will be fun to watch Connor and the Jets this season to see if they can finally finish that story, the one that ends with a trip to the Stanley Cup Final and maybe, just maybe, winning it all.

DID YOU KNOW?
Connor became the Jets' franchise leader in career shut-outs last season when he notched number 18 on January 14, 2020, against Vancouver. He added 2 more shut-outs before the end of the season, to give him a career total of 20 so far.

HOCKEY MEMORIES
Near Connor's childhood neighborhood was a rink on a little lake. There were lights, so they could play at night, but Connor had to try to put his equipment on in the dark. "I couldn't see a thing. I was just guessing. Not my fondest moment, but one I'll always remember."

2019–2020 STATS

GP	W	L	OT	GAA	SO
58	31	21	5	2.57	6

Winnipeg Jets' 4th choice, 130th overall, in 2012 NHL Entry Draft

1st NHL Team, Season: Winnipeg Jets, 2015–2016

Born: May 19, 1993, in Commerce, Michigan

Position: Goaltender

Catches: Left

Height: 1.93 m (6'4")

Weight: 94 kg (207 lbs.)

QUINN HUGHES

Although last season was Quinn Hughes's rookie year in the NHL, his first NHL action came in the final few games of the 2018–2019 season, after his NCAA campaign was over. Those games were a little taste for him, his teammates and the fans.

> "He's a joy to watch and a joy to coach. We're lucky to have him."
> — Vancouver coach Travis Green

"Those games helped me wrap my head around what to expect and to have confidence in myself," says Quinn.

What was obvious during those first few NHL games was that one of the main ingredients of his game was exceptional skating ability.

"His feet are, arguably, the best I've ever seen," said teammate Troy Stecher after watching Quinn play a few games.

What makes him such a great skater? It's not just the speed. There are a lot of fast skaters in the NHL. There aren't as many who can also change direction sharply and quickly, going through traffic, at full speed. In the era of puck-carrying defensemen leading a team's breakouts, that type of skating skill makes Quinn a perfect fit for the modern NHL game.

He also has great vision on the power play. His ability to either get the puck on net or to find the open man landed him on Vancouver's top power play unit. He ended up leading all rookies in power play scoring, with 25 points (3 goals, 22 assists).

It turned out that the little taste of Quinn's speed and skill fans got at the end of the 2018–2019 season was just the first course of a feast. He ripped through the league in his first season, leading all rookies with 45 assists and 53 points, and established a team record for assists by a rookie defenseman.

"You think you're going to do well, but you never know how things will go, so I'm humbled by that," said Quinn.

Quinn is already one of the best defensemen ever to wear a Canucks sweater. It's scary to think just how good he could get with a little more seasoning.

DID YOU KNOW?

Quinn became only the sixth rookie defenseman in Canucks history to record a multi-goal game, and only the second to have one of those goals be the game-winner. He pulled this off on February 1, 2020, against the New York Islanders.

HOCKEY MEMORIES

Although he was born in the U.S., Quinn's early memories are centered around Toronto, where his dad worked as Director of Player Development for the Maple Leafs. "I can remember playing mini-sticks with William Nylander when he was at our house," recalls Quinn.

2019–2020 STATS

GP	G	A	PTS
68	8	45	53

Vancouver Canucks' 1st choice, 7th overall, in 2018 NHL Entry Draft
1st NHL Team, Season: Vancouver Canucks, 2019–2020
Born: October 14, 1999, in Orlando, Florida
Position: Defense
Shoots: Left
Height: 1.78 m (5'10")
Weight: 77 kg (170 lbs.)

TRISTAN JARRY

Last season was an important one for Pittsburgh goalie Tristan Jarry. Tristan was drafted in 2013 off of a strong season with the Edmonton Oil Kings in the Western Hockey League. He played the next two seasons in the WHL, helping Edmonton to a Memorial Cup Championship in 2014. He played most of the next four seasons with Pittsburgh's minor league team in Wilkes-Barre/Scranton. It looked as though he'd taken a step towards his dream of becoming an NHL goalie when he started 23 games with the Pens in 2017–2018. But the following year he found himself back in the minors. On top of all of that, Tristan entered last season in the final year of his contract. The stage was set: 2019–2020 was going to be a big year.

"I guess it was just proving to myself that I could still put in the work and be able to do it at a high level. That was the big thing for me, just pushing myself to be better every day."

"When I did get sent down, I wanted to improve," reflected Tristan. "I wanted to come back better and stronger and make sure that, the next time I had an opportunity, I was making the most of it."

Tristan made the Pens out of camp as the back-up to Matt Murray. But in early December Murray faltered and Tristan stepped in and stepped up. Between then and the end of January, Tristan started 17 of 24 games, winning 12 of those starts.

A highlight for him last season was a trip to the NHL All-Star Game. Think about that: in January 2019 he was in the minors, the third goalie in the Pittsburgh depth chart. A year later he was representing the team at the All-Star Game.

"Having my parents there, and being able to share that with them, and having my whole family able to watch, it was an unforgettable moment and something that we'll cherish as a family forever."

Last season was an important one for Tristan Jarry, and he delivered. But he knows that, in the sports world, last season doesn't matter much once you hit the start of the next. What Tristan also knows, after last season, is that he belongs in the NHL.

DID YOU KNOW?

At one point last season Tristan picked up three shut-outs in four starts for a franchise-record shut-out streak of 177 minutes, 15 seconds.

HOCKEY MEMORIES

"The Memorial Cup is the pinnacle of junior hockey. I don't think we were one of the strongest teams, we were just the team that came together the fastest and we were able to continue that through the year we won."

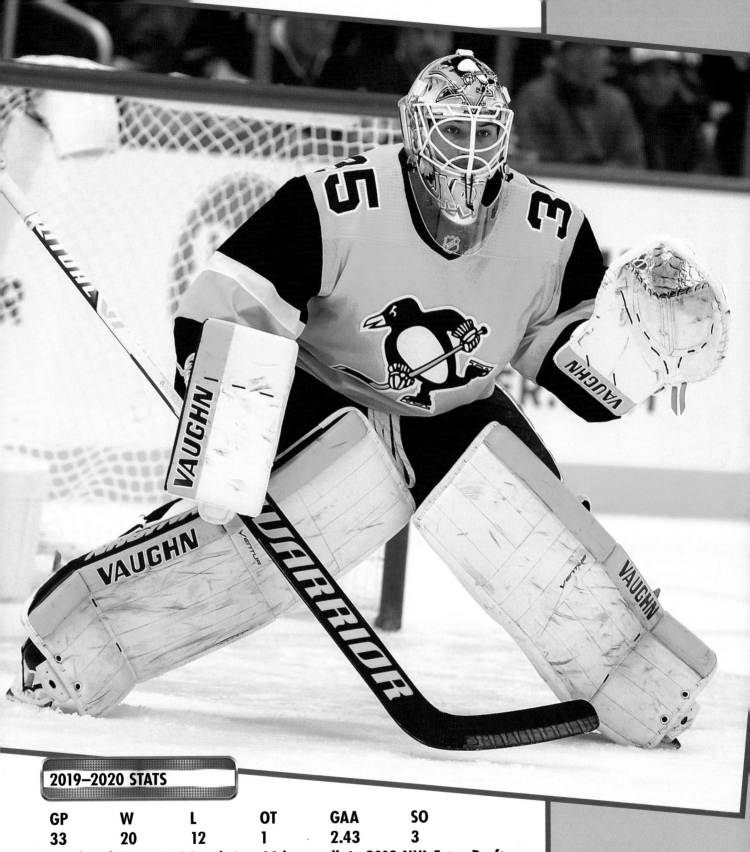

2019–2020 STATS

GP	W	L	OT	GAA	SO
33	20	12	1	2.43	3

Pittsburgh Penguins' 1st choice, 44th overall, in 2013 NHL Entry Draft

1st NHL Team, Season: Pittsburgh Penguins, 2017–2018

Born: April 29, 1995, in Surrey, British Columbia

Position: Goaltender

Catches: Left

Height: 1.88 m (6'2")

Weight: 88 kg (194 lbs.)

ELIAS LINDHOLM

The trade that brought Elias Lindholm from the Carolina Hurricanes to the Calgary Flames during the 2018 off-season was the best thing that could have happened, though it probably didn't feel that way. It's rarely fun being traded. Elias had been in Carolina since the start of his NHL career in 2013. But the reality was that he was becoming a restricted free agent and he and the Hurricanes were pretty far apart on agreeing to a new deal. He was told to expect a trade.

"If you start looking towards the numbers, you might start struggling a bit. I try to take it day by day and not force anything. If they go in, they go in."

"I was back home in Sweden, going to Calle Jarnkrok's house [Jarnkrok, a fellow NHLer, is Elias's cousin and close friend] to watch a World Cup match. He told me he had seen on Twitter that I'd been traded," recalls Elias.

Then came the phone calls and the questions and, eventually, the move to Calgary. And what a great move it has turned out to be. Elias, always an offensively gifted player, finally started finishing on the many goal-scoring chances he was able to generate. In his last two seasons in Calgary he has scored 56 goals, more than he managed in the previous four seasons with Carolina. Those numbers came as a surprise to some.

"If you don't get a chance to see him play that often then maybe you don't recognize just how good he is," says Jarnkrok. "But he's not just good offensively, he's also good defensively. He's such a well-rounded player."

Versatility is a good word to describe Elias's game. In his first season with the Flames he was mostly on right wing. Last season he was mostly at center. He plays the power play, but also the penalty kill.

"His offensive production doesn't suffer with what he does away from the puck," says Flames head coach Geoff Ward. "He's married the offensive and defensive parts of his game really well. He's one of our most consistent players."

Few things in the NHL are a guarantee, but it seems like a good bet that Elias won't have to deal with another off-season move anytime soon. He's right at home in Calgary.

DID YOU KNOW?

Elias was the youngest Swedish-born player to score a goal in the NHL. He was 18 years and 311 days old on October 10, 2013, when he scored his first career goal, bettering Gabriel Landeskog's previous record by 13 days.

HOCKEY MEMORIES

When he was 10, you wouldn't have found Elias patrolling center or a wing; you have found him playing goal. "It was cool and pretty fun," recalls Elias, "but at the end of the day I decided that it was more fun to score goals and help the team that way than getting hit by pucks."

2019–2020 STATS

GP	G	A	PTS
70	29	25	54

Carolina Hurricanes' 1st choice, 5th overall, in 2013 NHL Entry Draft
1st NHL Team, Season: Carolina Hurricanes, 2013–2014
Born: December 2, 1994, in Boden, Sweden
Position: Center
Shoots: Right
Height: 1.85 m (6'1")
Weight: 88.5 kg (195 lbs.)

There are many traits that superstar NHL players share, other than the obvious ones like talent, skill and being in great physical shape. Superstar players tend to be ultra-competitive and very demanding. They demand a lot from themselves and also from their teammates. Nathan MacKinnon is one of those players. He works as hard or harder than any player in the game and he expects the best out of himself. But he also expects fellow players to work just as hard.

> "I kind of hit a crossroads in my career when I was, like, 21, and we came in last place. I felt like I had to decide whether I wanted to be a decent player or a great player. I felt like I had a lot more to give than I was giving at the time."

"He puts in a lot of work, hours and hours, to prepare himself and make sure he's as good as he can be," says Colorado captain Gabriel Landeskog. "And he expects that from his teammates and his coaches and the organization. That's an important part of a team, to have a guy like that."

Nathan was the first overall pick in the 2013 NHL Entry Draft and Colorado made the playoffs in his rookie season, but the team sat at home for the next three post-seasons. Although Nathan won the Calder Trophy as NHL Rookie of the Year in 2014, his play, like the team's, became inconsistent.

Then came the 2017–2018 campaign. It all seemed to come together for the young superstar as he put up his best season ever with 97 points (39 goals, 58 assists) and finished second in balloting for the Hart Trophy as NHL MVP. He followed that up with seasons of 99 and 93 points. What a transformation. First four NHL seasons: 206 points. Last three seasons: 289. Along with that have come expectations.

"I think everyone here wants to be on a team where the Stanley Cup is the expectation," says Nathan matter-of-factly. "On good teams, playoffs are a given. You make the playoffs to win the Cup, not just to make the playoffs and give yourself a pat on the back."

Nathan expects nothing less from his teammates and himself than total commitment to winning it all.

DID YOU KNOW?

Nathan is the first player in Colorado Avalanche history to record three 90+ point seasons in a row. The great Peter Forsberg recorded back-to-back 90+ point seasons in 1997–1998 and 1998–1999.

HOCKEY MEMORIES

One of Nathan's earliest hockey memories is skating on a pond near where he grew up in Nova Scotia. His dad had Nathan on skates by the time he was two years old and says, "He took to it so well that I could barely keep up with him."

2019–2020 STATS

GP	G	A	PTS
69	35	58	93

Colorado Avalanche's 1st choice, 1st overall, in 2013 NHL Entry Draft

1st NHL Team, Season: Colorado Avalanche, 2013–2014

Born: September 1, 1995, in Halifax, Nova Scotia

Position: Center

Shoots: Right

Height: 1.83 m (6'0")

Weight: 91 kg (200 lbs.)

CALE MAKAR

Last season was the season of rookie defensemen in the NHL. Vancouver had the brilliant Quinn Hughes and Colorado countered with the equally sensational Cale Makar. Both hit the 50-point mark in their debut season, the first time in NHL history that the first two rookies to hit that mark were defensemen. Cale managed the feat in Colorado's final game of the shortened year, when he assisted on all three Colorado goals in a 3–2 win over the New York Rangers. His accomplishment was impressive to start with, but was made even more so considering he had missed 13 games with an upper-body injury.

> **"The sky is really the limit. He has been important for our team, no doubt. It is pretty impressive when you see him step into the NHL and the skill set that he has already."**
> **— Colorado captain Gabriel Landeskog**

Anyone who was surprised by Cale's success in his first NHL season wasn't paying much attention to the 2019 playoffs. Cale wrapped up his college hockey career with the Hobey Baker Award as the top player in U.S. college hockey. He then signed a three-year entry-level deal with Colorado and immediately joined the team for their first-round playoff series against the Calgary Flames. He scored the game-winner in his first game, the first time in NHL history that a defenseman made his league debut in the playoffs and scored a goal. Cale went on to record a goal and 5 assists in 10 post-season games, making him the second-highest scoring defenseman on the Avalanche that post-season. All before he'd seen a single second of regular-season action in the NHL. Teammates and opponents were already impressed.

"His confidence and poise with the puck is something else," says Minnesota defenseman Matt Dumba, a friend since their youth hockey days in Calgary. "He's such a complete player and so much fun to watch that I sometimes get caught up in just watching him myself."

It remains to be seen whether a rivalry will develop between Cale and Vancouver's Quinn Hughes. Regardless, hockey fans will talk about the rookie seasons of both defensemen for many years.

DID YOU KNOW?

Cale was named for a former NHL player! His dad met Cale Hulse when Hulse was playing for the Calgary Flames. He was impressed enough that he was inspired to use "Cale" as his son's first name.

HOCKEY MEMORIES

A couple of Cale's big memories played out in the KeyBank Center in Buffalo. He won a gold medal with Team Canada at the 2018 World Junior Championships there. Just over a year later, he played in the 2019 NCAA championship game with UMass in that same arena.

2019–2020 STATS

GP	G	A	PTS
57	12	38	50

Colorado Avalanche's 1st choice, 4th overall, in 2017 NHL Entry Draft
1st NHL Team, Season: Colorado Avalanche, 2019–2020
Born: October 30, 1998, in Calgary, Alberta
Position: Defense
Shoots: Right
Height: 1.80 m (5'11")
Weight: 85 kg (187 lbs.)

TORONTO MAPLE LEAFS

Expectations were always high for Toronto superstar Auston Matthews. Auston was taken first overall in the 2016 NHL Entry Draft, and he met all those expectations by scoring four goals in his NHL debut and never looking back on the way to winning the Calder Trophy as the Rookie of the Year.

His point total dropped ever so slightly in his second season when he missed 20 games with some minor injuries and a concussion. But, since then, he's scored at an incredible pace. Last season, despite it being cut short, Auston put up career highs in goals and points. He was on pace to score 50 goals and take a run at the Toronto franchise record of 54 goals in a season (Rick Vaive, 1981–1982).

"He's an amazing player and he's right at the top of his game. It's fun just to watch and be a part of," says teammate Tyson Barrie.

> "He has been an elite player since he came into the league and I think he has got better every year, which is hard to do when you're playing at that level."
> — Toronto teammate Zach Hyman

An extra element that Auston added to his game last season was a better one-timer. That's the type of shot where you take the pass and fire towards the goal without stopping the puck to control it first.

"You try to work on [one-timers] all the time in practice," says Auston. "You try to pick spots, try different shots, hand position on the stick, different things. It's definitely something I want to improve in my game."

Many of those chances come on the power play, and Auston's power play time — and points — went up last season after Sheldon Keefe took over as Toronto head coach. The prior season, under coach Mike Babcock, Auston played a total of 174 minutes on the power play. Last season he saw 223 minutes of ice time during the power play.

"I like to be out there as much as possible. I think that you always want to be better and want to constantly strive to improve," says Auston.

Spoken like a guy who works hard every season to meet people's expectations. So far, so incredible.

DID YOU KNOW?

Auston topped the 30-goal mark in each of his first four NHL seasons. No other Leafs player has done that. In the history of the NHL, only 15 players have managed the feat.

HOCKEY MEMORIES

Auston first played the game at an indoor place in Arizona with one small synthetic rink and one real ice rink. The games were all 3-on-3 and when his team wasn't playing, he'd hang around waiting to see if players on other teams didn't show up so he could jump in with them.

2019–2020 STATS

GP	G	A	PTS
70	47	33	80

Toronto Maple Leafs' 1st choice, 1st overall, in 2016 NHL Entry Draft

1st NHL Team, Season: Toronto Maple Leafs, 2016-2017

Born: September 17, 1997, in San Ramon, California

Position: Center

Shoots: Left

Height: 1.90 m (6'3")

Weight: 100 kg (220 lbs.)

ARTEMI PANARIN

It has taken a few seasons for Artemi Panarin to relax and let the pressure of trying to make his mark on the NHL dissolve away. When he moved from Russia to Chicago in 2015, he was adjusting to a new team, a new league and a new country.

> "He challenges you to be better based on how skilled he is."
> — New York teammate Ryan Strome

"The biggest things I notice in my first year in the NHL are the speed of the game and how much better people play without the puck," said Artemi at the time.

Artemi handled that first season's pressure extremely well. He ripped it up with 30 goals and 47 assists and was named the Calder Trophy winner as the NHL Rookie of the Year.

There was more pressure in 2017 when the Blackhawks traded him to the Columbus Blue Jackets. And then, you would think, even more a couple of seasons later when he left Columbus as a free agent and signed a multi-year deal with the New York Rangers. But hold on. According to Artemi, that last part isn't quite right.

"For sure I felt pressure when I arrived in Chicago," says Artemi. "And I put a lot of pressure on myself after I was traded by Chicago to Columbus. But here, in New York, I don't feel that pressure."

Perhaps that's because he's become more comfortable living in a new country, and most importantly, he's proven to himself and the rest of the league that he can deliver the goods consistently. He was the NHL's top rookie. He set a team record for most points in a single season when he was with Columbus. Then, last season, Artemi set career-high marks in goals, assists and points. He also added to his growing reputation as one of the great passers in the game right now.

"The guy's passing is off the charts," says teammate Chris Kreider. "He never looks at who he's passing to. It's all no look, and then it's sauce, right on the stick. And he's doing this in the best league in the world."

And Artemi Panarin wants to be the best player in the best league. No pressure there at all. Or if there is, he doesn't seem to feel it.

DID YOU KNOW?

Artemi picked up the nickname "Breadman" during his rookie season. Coach Joel Quenneville thought Panarin's last name sounded like the name of a chain of bakeries called Panera Bread.

HOCKEY MEMORIES

A cherished memory for Artemi was not only playing for Russia in the 2011 World Junior Championships, but scoring a pair of goals, including the game-winner, in a dramatic third period come-from-behind victory against Canada.

2019–2020 STATS

GP	G	A	PTS
69	32	63	95

Signed as a free agent by Chicago Blackhawks, May 1, 2015
1st NHL Team, Season: Chicago Blackhawks, 2015–2016
Born: October 30, 1991, in Korkino, USSR (now Russia)
Position: Left Wing
Shoots: Right
Height: 1.80 m (5'11")
Weight: 77 kg (170 lbs.)

DAVID PASTRNAK

Last season's unexpected end also brought an end to a great battle for the league scoring title. In one corner, the eight-time NHL goal-scoring champion, Washington's Alex Ovechkin. In the other, looking for his first crown, Boston's David Pastrnak. In the end the two finished tied, with 48 goals each.

"We've played together for a long time and they've been in the league for a while. They've won a Cup, so they know what it takes, and it's been easy for me to listen to them and get better every day."
— David on playing on Boston's top line

"I really wasn't racing with [Ovechkin]," said David. "I'm just going out and playing hockey. I'm trying to help my team win. I get paid to score. That's my biggest strength. But I'm not worrying about the scoring race."

It was a career-best season right across the board for the man teammates call "Pasta" — with career highs in goals, assists and points. There is little doubt that, with 12 games remaining in the season, he would have topped the 100-point mark. He scored goals often and in bunches, leading the Bruins with four hat tricks.

The line of Pastrnak, Brad Marchand and Patrice Bergeron is regarded by many as the best in the game, accounting for 238 of the Bruins' 607 combined points. As a result, it drew a lot of attention from the other teams' best defensive players. Since David was the top goal scorer on the line, he was often the focus of very physical play from opponents. Did that bother David?

"Not a bit. That's hockey. I get frustrated when we lose. That's it."

That comment is typical of David's attitude. He was taught a lot about the game and how to approach it by his late father, Milan. He learned to work hard at what he does, and to enjoy it. Adversity bounces off of him. He focuses on the positives. He absolutely loves to play and you can see it with almost every shot he fires and rush he takes in a game or practice. That approach has served him well so far, and you get the feeling it may well see him with his name on a few trophies before his career wraps up.

DID YOU KNOW?
During last year's season pause, David hosted a Q and A on Instagram. What did fans find out? That he has a dog named Eko and that the favorite pasta of the guy called "Pasta" is spaghetti carbonara.

HOCKEY MEMORIES
"Growing up as a kid in the Czech Republic, you would have ice from 11 a.m. to 12 p.m. You had to be there at 11 and get off right at 12. The NHL is the best. For practice you can go as early as you want and stay as long as you want."

2019–2020 STATS

GP	G	A	PTS
70	48	47	95

Boston Bruins' 1st choice, 25th overall, in 2014 NHL Entry Draft
1st NHL Team, Season: Boston Bruins, 2014–2015
Born: May 25, 1996, in Havířov, Czech Republic
Position: Right Wing
Shoots: Right
Height: 1.83 m (6'0")
Weight: 88 kg (194 lbs.)

STEVEN STAMKOS

TAMPA BAY LIGHTNING

When you look at the 2010s — seasons 2010–2011 through 2019–2020 — Steven Stamkos stands out as one of the superstars. Steven racked up some impressive accomplishments over those 10 years: he scored 348 goals, second only to Alex Ovechkin's mind-blowing total of 437; won the Rocket Richard Trophy as the league's top goal scorer; played in the Eastern Conference Final four times and the Stanley Cup Final once; and appeared in six All-Star Games. The glaring omission on that list is a Stanley Cup, and that's something he continues to work for.

"Every year that passes and you don't win, it's another opportunity that's gone. You want to take advantage of playing on a team of this caliber. The search for that elusive trophy continues, and you just want to do whatever you can to win."

Steven hit a couple of milestones last season. He scored his 400th career goal and played in his 800th career game. His 400th goal came in his 763rd game. Among active players, only Ovechkin reached the 400-goal mark more quickly.

"It's pretty surreal," Steven said.

"You never envision scoring that many goals in the NHL. Hopefully, many more to come."

Last season was cut short for Steven at the end of February by a muscle injury that required surgery. When he went down, Steven had scored at least a point in each of his last 15 games. The injury was, unfortunately, the latest of several Steven has had to work through during his career. Having had to play through and recover from them has left him with an appreciation for enjoying things when they are going well.

"Enjoy every moment and realize just how fortunate you are to be in the position you're in," Steven said last season. "You're not always going to feel like you're 21. I've had to deal with some injuries. So just have fun, and you just never know what's going to happen."

Of the two great goal scorers of the last decade, one — Ovechkin — finally got his name on the Cup in 2018. The hockey world awaits to see whether the other great goal scorer of the last 10 years will also have his name etched onto hockey's greatest prize.

DID YOU KNOW?
Steven and his wife, Sandra, welcomed their first child prior to the start of last season. The experience has been a great one so far. "I certainly have a new appreciation for all of the mothers in the world, that's for sure."

HOCKEY MEMORIES
Steven remembers accidentally shooting a puck through a car windshield when he was 12. He can't remember what kind of car it was, but he remembers being pretty nervous about having to tell the car's owner!

2019–2020 STATS

GP	G	A	PTS
57	29	37	66

Tampa Bay Lightning's 1st choice, 1st overall, in 2008 NHL Entry Draft
1st NHL Team, Season: Tampa Bay Lightning, 2008–2009
Born: February 7, 1990, in Markham, Ontario
Position: Center
Shoots: Right
Height: 1.85 m (6'1")
Weight: 88 kg (194 lbs.)

SHEA WEBER

As much as Shea Weber is looked up to for his play over the course of an almost 1000-game career (that mark will be passed early in the 2020–2021 campaign), he's equally revered for his leadership ability.

"You just need to set a good example: come in, work hard and be a good pro. Do the right things every day. You don't cheat on it. You don't skip on anything."

Here's a great example. On February 4 of last season, with Montreal in the thick of a battle for a playoff spot, Shea hurt his left ankle during a game against the New Jersey Devils. Eight days later, the Montreal Canadiens announced that Shea would be out from four to six weeks as a result of the injury. Four days after that announcement, Shea was back in the lineup, putting in his usual 25 to 30 shifts and 20-plus minutes of ice time. The most important reason was that he felt well enough to play. But just as important to him was knowing that the team needed him in the lineup for some big games.

"I know it might be a long shot [for us to make the playoffs], but there is still belief in here and I want to be part of that. I don't want to just sit back and watch," said Shea to a crowd of reporters after his sooner-than-expected return to the lineup.

"I don't think any of us expected to see him for a month," said teammate Nick Suzuki. "He's probably not at a hundred percent, but he wants to be battling with the rest of us. He's our leader and he sets an example for everyone who's here."

There are countless other tales of Shea's leadership from his time in Montreal and, before that, 11 seasons with the Nashville Predators: the new and younger teammates he's gone out of his way to make feel welcome in their new surroundings, and the team dinners he organizes to make sure guys are all pulling together and watching out for one another. And, like last season, playing through some pain because he knew the team needed him in the lineup.

"He does the right things, on the ice and off the ice, day after day," says teammate Brendan Gallagher.

Off the ice, on the ice, Shea Weber is a leader.

DID YOU KNOW?

Entering the 2020–2021 season, Shea leads all active defensemen in both regular-season goals, with 218, and power play goals, with 102.

HOCKEY MEMORIES

Shea played for the Canadian Olympic Hockey Team that won gold in 2010 in Vancouver. "It was so close to home for me. I had all my family there. My mom and grandpa and people that aren't with us now were there and got to enjoy that special moment. That sticks out for me."

GP	G	A	PTS
65	15	21	36

Nashville Predators' 4th choice, 49th overall, in 2003 NHL Entry Draft
1st NHL Team, Season: Nashville Predators, 2005–2006
Born: August 14, 1985, in Sicamous, British Columbia
Position: Defense
Shoots: Right
Height: 1.93m (6'4")
Weight: 104.5 kg (230 lbs.)

REFEREE SIGNALS

Do you know what is happening when the referee stops play and makes a penalty call? If you don't, then you're missing an important part of the game. The referee can call different penalties that result in anything from playing a man short for two minutes to having a player kicked out of the game.

Here are some of the most common referee signals. Now you'll know what penalties are being called against your team.

Cross-checking
Striking an opponent with the stick, while both hands are on the stick and both arms are extended.

Boarding
Checking an opponent into the boards in a violent way.

Charging
Checking an opponent in a violent way as a result of skating or charging at him.

Elbowing
Checking an opponent with an elbow.

High-sticking
Striking an opponent with the stick, which is held above shoulder height.

Holding
Holding back an opponent with the hands or arms.

Hooking
Using the blade of the stick to hold back an opponent.

Icing
Shooting the puck across the opposing team's goal line from one's own side of the rink. Called only if the opposing player touches the puck first.

Interference
Holding back an opponent who does not have the puck in play.

Kneeing
Using a knee to hold back an opponent.

Misconduct
A ten-minute penalty — the longest type called. Usually for abuse of an official.

Roughing
Shoving or striking an opponent.

REFEREE SIGNALS

Slashing
Using the stick to strike an opponent.

Spearing
Poking an opponent with the blade of the stick.

Slow whistle
The official waits to blow his whistle because of a delayed offside or delayed penalty call. Done while the opposing team has control of the puck.

Tripping
Tripping an opponent with the stick, a hand or a foot.

Unsportsmanlike conduct
Showing poor sportsmanship toward an opponent. For example: biting, pulling hair, etc.

Wash-out
Goal not allowed.

FINAL TEAM STANDINGS 2019–2020

EASTERN CONFERENCE
Atlantic Division

Team	GP	W	L	OT	PTS
BOSTON	70	44	14	12	100
TAMPA BAY	70	43	21	6	92
TORONTO	70	36	25	9	81
FLORIDA	69	35	26	8	78
MONTREAL	71	31	31	9	71
BUFFALO	69	30	31	8	68
OTTAWA	71	25	34	12	62
DETROIT	71	17	49	5	39

Metropolitan Division

Team	GP	W	L	OT	PTS
WASHINGTON	69	41	20	8	90
PHILADELPHIA	69	41	21	7	89
PITTSBURGH	69	40	23	6	86
CAROLINA	68	38	25	5	81
NY ISLANDERS	68	35	23	10	80
COLUMBUS	70	33	22	15	81
NY RANGERS	70	37	28	5	79
NEW JERSEY	69	28	29	12	68

WESTERN CONFERENCE
Pacific Division

Team	GP	W	L	OT	PTS
VEGAS	71	39	24	8	86
EDMONTON	71	37	25	9	83
VANCOUVER	69	36	27	6	78
CALGARY	70	36	27	7	79
ARIZONA	70	33	29	8	74
ANAHEIM	71	29	33	9	67
LOS ANGELES	70	29	35	6	64
SAN JOSE	70	29	36	5	63

Central Division

Team	GP	W	L	OT	PTS
ST LOUIS	71	42	19	10	94
COLORADO	70	42	20	8	92
DALLAS	69	37	24	8	82
NASHVILLE	69	35	26	8	78
WINNIPEG	71	37	28	6	80
MINNESOTA	69	35	27	7	77
CHICAGO	70	32	30	8	72

GP = Games played; W = Wins; L = Losses; OT = Overtime losses; PTS = Points

Top Ten Points Leaders 2019–2020

PLAYER	TEAM	GP	G	A	P	S	S%
1 LEON DRAISAITL	EDMONTON	71	43	67	110	218	19.7
2 CONNOR McDAVID	EDMONTON	64	34	63	97	212	16.0
3 DAVID PASTRNAK	BOSTON	70	48	47	95	279	17.2
4 ARTEMI PANARIN	NY RANGERS	69	32	63	95	209	15.3
5 NATHAN MacKINNON	COLORADO	69	35	58	93	318	11.0
6 BRAD MARCHAND	BOSTON	70	28	59	87	185	15.1
7 NIKITA KUCHEROV	TAMPA BAY	68	33	52	85	210	15.7
8 PATRICK KANE	CHICAGO	70	33	51	84	275	12.0
9 AUSTON MATTHEWS	TORONTO	70	47	33	80	290	16.2
10 JACK EICHEL	BUFFALO	68	36	42	78	227	15.9

GP = Games played; G = Goals; A = Assists; P = Points;
S = Shots; S% = Percentage

Top Ten Goalies — Total Wins 2019–2020

PLAYER	TEAM	GP	W	L	OT	SA%	GA	GAA
1 ANDREI VASILEVSKIY	TAMPA BAY	52	35	14	3	0.917	133	2.56
2 CONNOR HELLEBUYCK	WINNIPEG	58	31	21	5	0.922	140	2.57
3 JORDAN BINNINGTON	ST LOUIS	50	30	13	7	0.912	126	2.56
4 FREDERIK ANDERSEN	TORONTO	52	29	13	7	0.909	143	2.85
5 CAREY PRICE	MONTREAL	58	27	25	6	0.909	160	2.79
6 MARC-ANDRE FLEURY	VEGAS	49	27	16	5	0.905	133	2.77
7 TUUKKA RASK	BOSTON	41	26	8	6	0.929	85	2.12
8 BRADEN HOLTBY	WASHINGTON	48	25	14	6	0.897	142	3.11
9 CARTER HART	PHILADELPHIA	43	24	13	3	0.914	95	2.42
10 DAVID RITTICH	CALGARY	48	24	17	6	0.907	138	2.97

GP = Games played; W = Wins; L = Losses; OT = Overtime and/or Shut-Out Losses;
SA% = Save percentage; GA = Goals Against; GAA = Goals-Against Average

END-OF-SEASON STATS

Countdown to the Cup 2020–2021

EASTERN CONFERENCE

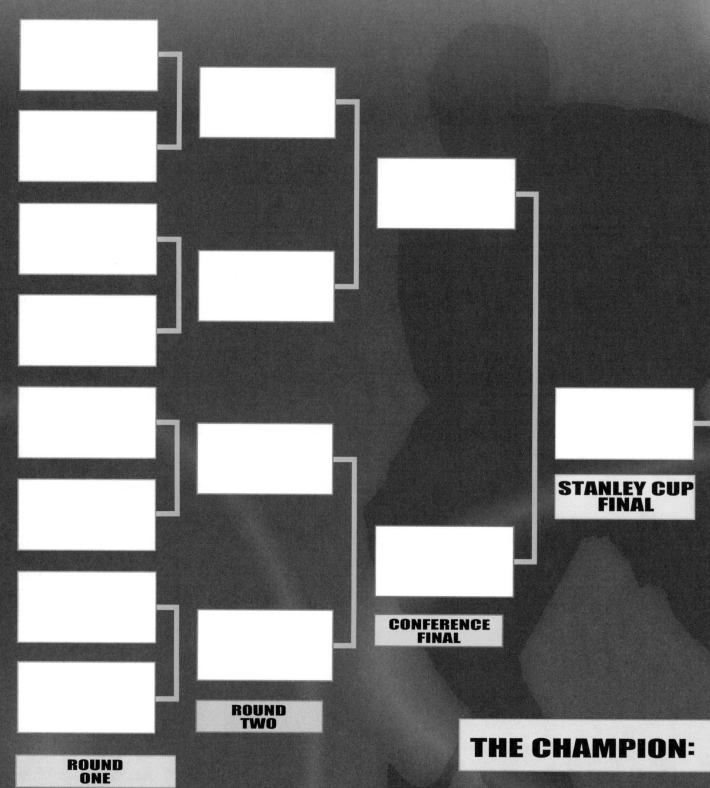

ROUND ONE

ROUND TWO

CONFERENCE FINAL

STANLEY CUP FINAL

THE CHAMPION:

WESTERN CONFERENCE

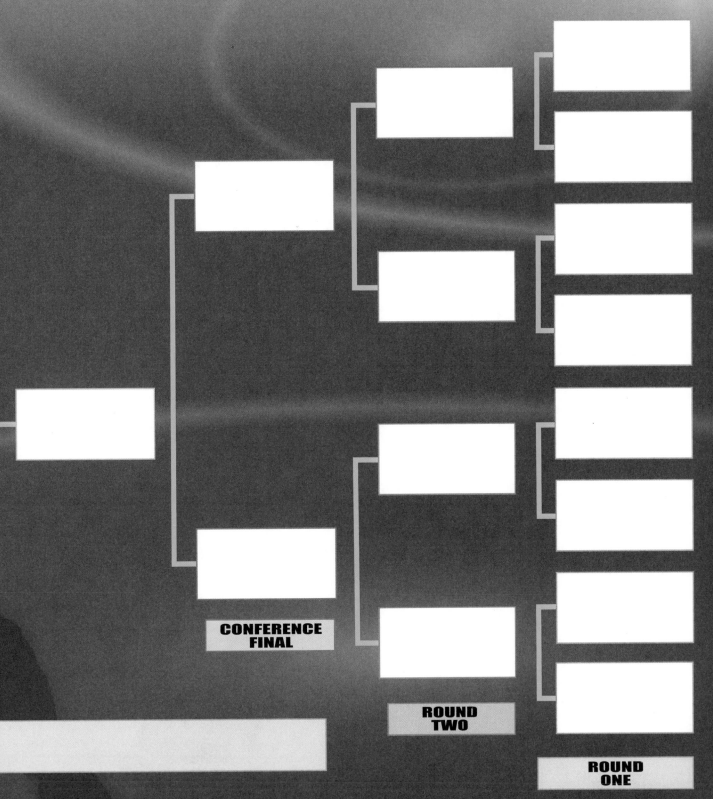

CONFERENCE
FINAL

ROUND
TWO

ROUND
ONE

NHL AWARDS

Here are some of the major NHL awards for individual players. Go to www.scholastic.ca/hockey-superstars to find all the 2020 award winners, then fill in your guesses for 2021. At the end of the season, see how many you got right.

HART MEMORIAL TROPHY
Awarded to the player judged to be the most valuable to his team. Selected by the Professional Hockey Writers Association.

2020 winner: _____

Your choice for 2021: _____

The winner: _____

ART ROSS TROPHY
Awarded to the player who leads the league in scoring points at the end of the regular season.

2020 winner: **Leon Draisaitl**

Your choice for 2021: _____

The winner: _____

CALDER MEMORIAL TROPHY
Awarded to the player selected as the most proficient in his first year of competition in the NHL. Selected by the Professional Hockey Writers Association.

2020 winner: _____

Your choice for 2021: _____

The winner: _____

JAMES NORRIS TROPHY
Awarded to the defense player who demonstrates throughout his season the greatest all-round ability. Selected by the Professional Hockey Writers Association.

2020 winner: _____

Your choice for 2021: _____

The winner: _____

VEZINA TROPHY
Awarded to the goalkeeper judged to be the best. Selected by the NHL general managers.

2020 winner: _____

Your choice for 2021: _____

The winner: _____

MAURICE RICHARD TROPHY

Awarded to the player who scores the highest number of regular-season goals.

2020 winner: **Alex Ovechkin and David Pastrnak**

Your choice for 2021: _____

The winner: _____

WILLIAM M. JENNINGS TROPHY

Awarded to the goalkeeper(s) who played a minimum of 25 games for the team with the fewest goals scored against it.

2020 winner: **Tuukka Rask and Jaroslav Halak**

Your choice for 2021: _____

The winner: _____

LADY BYNG MEMORIAL TROPHY

Awarded to the player judged to have exhibited the best sportsmanship combined with a high standard of playing ability. Selected by the Professional Hockey Writers Association.

2020 winner: _____

Your choice for 2021: _____

The winner: _____

FRANK J. SELKE TROPHY

Awarded to the forward who best excels in the defensive aspects of the game. Selected by the Professional Hockey Writers Association.

2020 winner: _____

Your choice for 2021: _____

The winner: _____

CONN SMYTHE TROPHY

Awarded to the player most valuable to his team in the Stanley Cup playoffs. Selected by the Professional Hockey Writers Association.

2020 winner: _____

Your choice for 2021: _____

The winner: _____

BILL MASTERTON MEMORIAL TROPHY

Awarded to the player who best exemplifies the qualitites of perseverance, sportsmanship and dedication to hockey. Selected by the Professional Hockey Writers Association.

2020 winner: _____

Your choice for 2021: _____

The winner: _____

FUTURE STARS?

Drafting players for NHL teams is a tough job. For example, of the 210 players taken in the 2010 NHL Entry Draft, only 60 (28.6%) have played 120 or more games in the NHL. One hundred and three of the players drafted (49%) didn't play a single NHL game. It can be a bit of a guessing game, but here are some players we think will make the grade and have long careers.

Alexis Lafrenière

ALEXIS LAFRENIÈRE

Left Wing
1.85 m (6'1") / 88 kg (193 lbs.)
Born: October 11, 2001, in Saint-Eustache, Quebec
2019–2020 Club: Rimouski Océanic, QMJHL

QUINTON BYFIELD

Center
1.93 m (6'4") / 97.5 kg (215 lbs.)
Born: August 19, 2002, in Newmarket, Ontario
2019–2020 Club: Sudbury Wolves, OHL

Quinton Byfield

JAMIE DRYSDALE

Defense
1.80 m (5'11") / 79 kg (175 lbs.)
Born: April 8, 2002, in Toronto, Ontario
2019–2020 Club: Erie Otters, OHL

Jamie Drysdale

TIM STÜETZLE

Left Wing
1.85 m (6'1") / 85 kg (187 lbs.)
Born: January 15, 2002, in Viersen, Germany
2019–2020 Club: Adler Mannheim, DEL
(German League)